KILLED. JULY 17TH 1916. A PLAY
FOR TOP SECONDARY PUPILS.
BELGRADE THEATRE IN EDUCATION

KILLED: July 17th 1916

Ration party resting in a communications trench, the Somme, July 1916.

KILLED:
July 17th 1916

A play for top secondary pupils

Belgrade Theatre in Education Company

AMBER LANE PRESS

Acknowledgement

Prologue: The Reality is reproduced with the kind permission of
the author, William Moore, and Frederick Warne (Publishers)
Limited. The story is one of a collection from *The Thin Yellow
Line* by William Moore (Leo Cooper Publishing, 1974).
All the photographs in this edition are reproduced with the kind
permission of the Imperial War Museum, London

All rights whatsoever in this play are strictly reserved and application for
performance etc. should be made before rehearsal to:
The Administrator,
Belgrade Theatre in Education Company,
The Belgrade Theatre,
Corporation Street,
Coventry CV1 1GS.
No performance may be given unless a licence has been obtained.
First published in 1982 by
Amber Lane Press Ltd.,
9a Newbridge Road,
Ambergate, Derbyshire DE5 2GR.
Printed in Great Britain by
Cotswold Press Ltd., Oxford.
Copyright © Belgrade Theatre in Education Company, 1982
Prologue: The Reality Copyright © William Moore, 1974
ISBN 0 906399 28 9

KILLED: July 17th 1916 was originally devised, researched and performed by members of the Belgrade Theatre in Education Company: Linda Bassett, Barbara Marten, Philip Whitchurch, Rob Bettinson, Fred Hawksley and Tony Flynn.

The first performance of the play was given on 6th December 1978 with the following cast:

BILLY DEAN:	Rob Bettinson
REGIMENTAL SERGEANT MAJOR:	Philip Whitchurch
TOMMY:	Tony Flynn
PRIVATE WALSH:	Tony Flynn
CAPTAIN HOWARD:	Tony Flynn
MAY DEAN:	Barbara Marten
ELSIE:	Linda Bassett
WOMAN:	Linda Bassett

Directed by Fred Hawksley
Set designed by Sue Mayes

CHARACTERS

BILLY DEAN:	Infantryman, 18th Manchesters (3rd Manchester Pals)
R.S.M.:	Regimental Sergeant Major
TOMMY:	Infantryman, 18th Manchesters
PRIVATE WALSH:	Infantryman, 18th Manchesters
CAPTAIN HOWARD:	Officer, 18th Manchesters
MAY DEAN:	Billy's wife
ELSIE:	Friend of Billy and May
WOMAN:	Upper-class patriot
SOLDIERS	

Waiting in the trenches.

INTRODUCTION
by members of Belgrade Theatre in Education Company

After the outbreak of war in 1914 the call went out all over Britain for volunteers to join the army. Thousands upon thousands of young men answered that call, leaving their homes, families and jobs to fight for their country. Many of them had lived their whole lives in harsh conditions and dreadful poverty. Some of them had never before travelled outside their own home towns, let alone to France.

These men formed the famous 'Pals' battalions. They were friends, all from the same crowded streets, or the same factory or trade. They were taken away and trained to fight and were eventually forged into regiments of soldiers, linked by their community or by their work. They were proud and ready to fight. Their only anxiety was that the war would be over before they got there.

Britain had never seen anything like it. A spirit of optimism infected the whole country. Everybody said it: 'The war is sure to be over by Christmas.' Those staying behind gathered at the railway stations and ports to cheer the lads as they left for France.

For most of them there was to be no homecoming. The 'Great War' lasted for four years and a whole generation was cut to pieces and buried on the muddy battlefields of France.

Why did they go? What were they fighting for? What did they gain? Could such a thing happen today? Questions like these were ringing in our heads after only preliminary research. So we decided that we would attempt to devise a secondary programme dealing with the Great War.

Creating the play
Soon after starting detailed research in the autumn of 1978 it was obvious to us that any number of plays could be written on the subject, all with something vital to say.

At first we wanted to cover everything. We wanted people to see the young boys and old men lying about their age so as not to miss out on the action. We wanted to show the women back home, working night and day to keep 'Tommy' clothed, fed and armed so that he could fight the 'evil Hun'.

We wanted to show the thousands of men mown down in seconds like toy soldiers, in battles designed to gain only a few yards more of mud-filled trench. We wanted to show their spirit, the depth of feeling that each man had for his fellow, the camaraderie that kept them together through a living hell. We wanted to show the German and British soldiers playing football together during Christmas 1916, and being ordered back into the trenches to resume battle under the threat of being shelled by their own side.

We also wanted to show the unchallengable authority of the generals, making decisions that affected thousands of lives with a blind carelessness that only a strictly class-structured society could have accepted. And we wanted to show the brutal victimisation meted out by society to the conscientious objectors for deciding not to fight. Finally, we wanted people to see the return of the survivors, maimed and scarred, to a land that was not 'fit for heroes', as they had been led to believe.

We really would have liked to have shown it all, but that play had already taken place. The drama was played out with grim reality between the years 1914 and 1918. It involved a cast of millions and a great deal of wasted effort.

After much talking and a lot of varied improvisation, we chose to focus on a story that we found in a book called *The Thin Yellow Line* by William Moore. We knew that this had all the ingredients for a very fine TIE programme. Although at first it seemed a simple story, to us it encapsulated everything we wanted to express. All we had to do was to use our imagination, flesh it out with more research and bring the characters to life.

Prologue: The Reality is a story about people faced with personal dilemmas of loyalty and duty in an extreme situation that is too complex for them to comprehend. We could see that by involving the students with these people we could say a lot, not only about the Great War but about any war, and how people justify their individual actions in the immensity of a national conflict.

We began by researching the story in detail. With the help of the Imperial War Museum we managed to find out more about the 18th Manchester (3rd Manchester Pals): their basic composition, where they trained, and their movements whilst at home and abroad. We were able to find maps of the Somme battlefield and of Trônes Wood in particular, so by linking our story with other information gathered about the battle we could trace the steps of our main character, renamed Billy Dean. By absorbing a great deal of other background material on the period and then working through improvisation we created the characters and situations which formed themselves into a finished script six weeks after starting the research.

We devised the play as a vital, exciting and emotional stimulus so that students would become involved through identifying with the characters. This, we hoped, would encourage them to pursue various lines of follow-up work.

The response to the programme was indeed very positive and many students have done further work, not only on the historical aspects but also on the social implications of the material in relation to the present day.

As a company we were very pleased with *Killed* and it is a measure of its success that a number of other TIE teams around the country have since chosen to perform the play. From our experience in presenting it to adult audiences we have found that it works as successfully for them as it does for secondary school students.

Presenting the play

It is important to recognise that in the play there are two different time scales at work. The whole play takes place during a single night, that is the night before Billy Dean's execution. Throughout that night there is a rising tension in Billy, and the play gathers momentum as the execution approaches.

In the first half Billy is dumped in the barn after what must have been the most frightening experience of his life. His mind is in turmoil. He is facing death. He slowly starts to relive the different important events in his life leading up to his present predicament. Sometimes he consciously recalls these experiences, sometimes they force themselves upon him, catching him by surprise. These recollections are very personal to Billy and in presenting them one must strive to find the truth of how they related to him at the time and what they mean to him now as he is gradually coming to terms with his impending execution.

In the second half of the play the mood changes. Dawn is near. Billy has no more time for recollections. He has recognised that he has only a few hours left and he is trying to control his fears by writing all that he wants to say to his wife before it is too late. All the scenes take place in these same few hours. Billy, frantically scribbling his letter, is a constant presence.

The soldiers involved in the execution keep their own anxious vigil. Elsie and May, back home in the munitions factory, work out the last few hours of their shift. They counterpoint the tension with their unawareness of what is happening in France. The scenes cut together to build the tension up to the final moment when May's relieved laugh replaces the noise of the shots that kill her husband.

Notes on the characters

All the characters in the play are of a generation that has always believed in obedience and loyalty to the established order. They cannot question or challenge authority without experiencing a difficult internal struggle.

Billy Dean: 21 years old. He has always been ruled by his feelings. Thinking does not come easily to him. For the first time in his life he is alone and faced with something he has to struggle to work out for himself.

May Dean: About 20. She is a vigorous and sensitive young woman, with a strong sense of right and wrong which is deeply felt rather than consciously thought out.

R.S.M.: A man who really cares about the soldiers under him. He has learned some hard lessons and believes it is in their best interests that his men learn them too. The army is his life. It gives him the security and sense of purpose he needs. He has worked his way up from the lowest rank to the highly respected position of Regimental Sergeant Major.

Elsie: Slightly older than May. She is resilient but not hard. She has a need to think things out for herself, however difficult her life may become as a result. She and May are close friends and the relationship is important to them both.

Tommy: The same age as Billy. He is light-hearted, friendly and popular. He and Billy are mates.

Captain: A young man with a strong sense of duty and honour. The amount of responsibility that he shoulders is a burden to him. He would have been involved in the recent action.

Patriotic woman: The mother of a young soldier killed in the first few weeks of the war. She believes in what she says and has a genuine desire to communicate with her listeners.

Suggested background reading

All Quiet on the Western Front Erich Maria Remarque (Putnam, 1929; Mayflower, 1968)

Bells of Hell Go Ting-a-ling-a-ling Eric C. Hiscock (Arlington, 1976; Corgi 1977)

British Society and the First World War Arthur Marwick (Macmillan, 1973)

Dear Old Blighty E.S. Turner (Michael Joseph, 1980)

Death's Men: Soldiers of the Great War Denis Winter (Penguin, 1979)

Eye Deep in Hell John Ellis (Croom Helm, 1976)

First Day on the Somme Martin Middlebrook (Allen Lane, 1971)

First World War A.J.P. Taylor (Penguin, 1970)

Fourteen Eighteen John Masters (Michael Joseph, 1965)

History of World War I A.J.P. Taylor (Octopus, 1974)

Home Fronts: Britain, France and Germany 1914-1918 John Williams (Constable, 1972)

Illustrated History of the World Wars A.J.P. Taylor (Octopus, 1978)

Johnny Get Your Gun: Personal narrative of the Somme, Ypres and Arras John Tucker (Kimber, 1978)

Keep the Home Fires Burning: Propaganda in the First World War Cate Haste (Allen Lane, 1977)

March to Armistice, 1918 Christopher Haworth (Kimber, 1968)

Mud, Songs and Blighty: A scrapbook of the First World War Colin Walsh (Hutchinson, 1975)

A Pictorial History of the World War I Years Edward Jablonski (Doubleday, 1979)

Poetry of the First World War Dominic Hibberd (Macmillan, 1981)

Poor Bloody Infantry: A memoir of the First World War W.H.A. Groom (Kimber, 1976)

Psychological Warfare Charles Roetter (Batsford, 1974)

Road to Passchendaele John Terraine (Leo Cooper, 1977)

Scars Upon My Heart: Women's poetry and verse of the First World War Catherine Reilly (ed) (Virago, 1981)

Tommy Goes to War Malcolm Brown (Dent, 1978)

War and the Trenches Matthew Holden (Wayland, 1973)

War in the Trenches Alan Lloyd (Hart Davis, 1976)

War by Time-table A.J.P. Taylor (Macdonald, 1969)

Women at War, 1914-18 Arthur Marwick (Croom Helm/Fontana, 1977)

PROLOGUE: THE REALITY

For a terror-stricken boy in khaki the end was a kitchen chair hidden in a French quarry.

The men of the 18th Manchesters were glad to be leaving the crashing, flaring chalk uplands of the Somme. They had seen enough of them in the summer of 1916. As the cattle trucks rumbled through the night away from the pulverised villages and splintered woods most of them slept. Some sat and stared, with feverish eyes while a few talked of what they had been through. In one wagon, guards shared their food with a comrade who had been court martialled a short time previously. There was a good deal of chaff and banter. The prisoner had been remanded to await sentence and his captors reckoned that he would be kept on cookhouse fatigue or made sanitary man for 'the duration'. It was the sort of scene one might expect in a Pals battalion.

There was something special about these formations made up of the volunteers who responded to Kitchener's call in 1914. They were so much more than a processed wodge of patriotic ardour. They were real 'pals' — in the 18th (3rd Manchester Pals) all clerks and warehousemen. They had something to be proud of too. On 1 July, when so many other units had lost nearly all their men with little to show for it, the 30th Division, to which the Manchesters belonged, had notched up one of the rare successes of the day.

General Headquarters, which had expressed some doubts about the division before the battle, was delighted. Further deeds of valour were required of the three brigades, one Regular, one of Liverpool Pals battalions and the other of Manchesters. During the remainder of July they struggled to wrench the shattered copses of Trônes Wood and the tumbled ruins of Guillemont village from the Germans. It was in one of these gruelling actions that the prisoner disappeared from his platoon. When he reported after the attack he explained that he had become separated from his section during the confusion but had attached himself to a group of men from the 11th South Lancashire

Regiment, the divisional pioneers. He had not thought it necessary to get a note from the officer. And he was not sure exactly where he had been. After all he had been lost! When inquiries failed to trace any-one who could corroborate his story — hardly surprising under the circumstances — the soldier's position came under more serious scrutiny. He was 'put back' for court martial and duly tried for deser-tion in the face of the enemy. The prisoner told his story over and over again on the way from the front to the battalion's rest area. He was not a well-educated man, just an ordinary working lad who had been sent out with the first draft of reinforcements to join the battalion after it arrived in France in 1915. The general consensus opinion was that he would 'click' for the dirty jobs in the next few months.

The men who guarded the prisoner on the train were taken off escort duty at the end of the journey. When next they saw him they were standing with the rest of the battalion formed in a hollow square. They had been expecting to hear some new order or even an exhortation from the General read out. Instead a horse-drawn ambu-lance had driven up to a table in the centre of the square. The prisoner had been marched to a prominent position near the table where the officers were gathered, his hat had been removed brusquely by the Regimental Sergeant Major, and the adjutant had read out his sent-ence. His punishment, awarded by field general court martial and confirmed by the Commander-in-Chief, Sir Douglas Haig, was to be shot. The execution would take place the following morning at dawn. At the bark of the R.S.M. the prisoner wheeled about and vanished into the ambulance which rattled out of sight. The 18th Manchesters stood stunned. Faces remained blank but the eyes betrayed a hurt, questioning look. Under steel helmets brains were racing. They'd all heard announcements of the sort before but no-one had really believed them. After all, they were volunteers. They didn't have to be there. Even as they marched away there were plenty of men in the shabby khaki ranks who muttered about appeals and 'They're only doing it to frighten us.' But they were not in the little group which had been assembled immediately after the parade at which the sentence had been promulgated. This unhappy squad had known the serious nature of their errand the moment the captain told them in strangled tones, 'I only hope to God you shoot straight.'

There were, in addition to the officer, a sergeant and ten soldiers. Six of the men were to form the firing squad. The remaining four were to act as stretcher bearers and remove the corpse. The bearers collected a limber and twenty-four hours' rations for the party and drove to a small farm some distance away.

The prisoner was housed in a hut with a Military Policeman present at all times. Not far away the execution squad brewed tea in an old barn. They didn't have much appetite. It had been impossible to conceal their intentions from the farmer's family and from time to time the soldiers bumped into weeping daughters of the household. Not being able to explain to the women that they were only doing their duty and that to disobey orders would imperil their own lives made the situation even more harrowing. Someone asked a military policeman what 'he' was doing. 'Writing letters' was the reply.

At some point the padre arrived to see the prisoner and the firing squad were ordered out and marched to a quarry on the outskirts of the farm. A staff officer was waiting, the red band on his hat providing the only colour in an otherwise unutterably drab scene. The squad filed down steps cut into the side of the quarry and lined up with a lot of nervous shuffling, riflemen in front, the stretcher party immediately to their rear. As the staff officer engaged the captain in earnest conversation all eyes focused on a single object. Some eight or nine paces from the firing squad stood a heavy kitchen chair.

'The prisoner will be placed in that chair in the morning,' the staff officer announced when the squad had been called to attention. 'After you have been brought to the 'present' I will give the signal by dropping my handkerchief and you will fire at the mark. Is that clear?'

After a moment's pause a worried looking soldier coughed, swallowed and asked, 'Sir . . .'

'Yes, what is it?'

'Aa doon't think Aa should be on this duty. Aa know the prisoner well. We coom from the same town. And we're in t'same coompany.'

The staff officer and the captain exchanged glances. Then the Red Band made up his mind.

'I can understand your feelings,' he said. 'I am aware this is an unpleasant duty for all of you. It isn't pleasant for me either. But the responsibility it not yours. It lies elsewhere and you've got to obey orders. We all have. So I can make no exceptions. I'm afraid you will have to go through with it.'

The squad stood silent. The Manchester officer bit his lip.

'Right. Shall we try it now?'

The captain barked out the orders, six pairs of unwilling eyes stared down the barrels of six unloaded rifles aimed at an empty chair and an unharmonious clicking announced that six triggers had been squeezed in response to the dropped handkerchief.

After the staff officer had explained that six rifles would be issued the next morning, one of which would contain a blank round, the squad filed up the steps and back to the farm. In the deserted quarry dusk closed over the empty kitchen chair.

In the barn the night dragged interminably. A bottle of whisky had been sent to the condemned man but the guard reported that he had refused to touch it. He was continuing to write his letters. Even at this late hour he did not seem to comprehend his peril. Just before dawn the sergeant shook the dozing soldiers. Stiff and silent they made their way to the quarry filling their lungs with the damp air. A muffled rumble in the distance told them that the war was still going on where the sky was growing paler in the east. The hateful chair stood where they had left it, dark and ominous and damp with dew.

Many men are reported to have faced a firing squad bravely. This man, who had gone 'over the top' on 1 July and endured the terrors of Trônes Wood, was not one of them. The waiting Manchesters saw the shirt-sleeved figure sway at the top of the quarry steps and watched the escort almost carry him down. His body seemed to be rigid as he was dragged to the waiting chair and the Military Police had difficulty as they tied his limbs to the wooden legs and arms. Someone pinned a piece of white cloth over the man's chest and stepped back. In the anxiety to get the business over with the man had still not been blindfolded when the volley crashed out, its noise magnified by the quarry walls.

'Oh, my God!'

The victim's head had fallen to one side but it was obvious that he was still alive. Without bothering to consult the medical officer who had been present throughout the affair, the Manchester captain strode forward muttering between clenched teeth: 'I shall have to finish him off.' With an obvious effort of self-control he put his pistol to the dying man's ear and pulled the trigger.

As the white-faced bearers moved forward one of the Military Police muttered accusingly out of the side of his mouth: 'Your men's rifles were shaking.' But the little party could not take their eyes off the dead man. When they cut the limp arms free and pulled him from the chair one of them noticed that the dead man's hair was 'standing up stiff and straight from sheer terror'. After the firing squad and the officers had left, the heavy stretcher was manhandled up the quarry steps and placed in the waiting limber. At the cemetery near Bailleul-ment, where they had been instructed to bury the man, the bearer party discovered that nothing had been prepared. So they borrowed the tools and dug the grave themselves, wrapping the body in a water-proof cape. Some months later a visitor to the cemetery reported that the grave bore a cross but instead of the words 'Killed in action', as on similar crosses, it merely said 'Killed' along with the date of the execution. Nothing else.

On the afternoon of the execution the burial detail returned to their billets and, under the gaze of their comrades, swilled the blood off the stretcher. Some of the watchers looked puzzled and resentful. Only eighteen months earlier, Sir Douglas Haig had listed the 18th Manchesters in his despatches as among units which had been 'specially brought to my notice for good work in carrying out or repelling local attacks and raids'. Now the battalion would be associated with the execution when it was announced on parades or published in Orders. Both the praise in the despatch and the rebuke implied in the report of the death sentence were essential, it seemed, for the maintenance of good order and discipline . . . but no-one could quite see why.

[Compiled from an eye-witness account given by P.J. Kennedy, a former private in the 18th Manchester Regiment and Military Medal holder.]

Action of Outtersteene Ridge, Meteren, August 1918.

ACT ONE

The lights are dim. The R.S.M. *comes in through the door. He checks out the room.*

R.S.M.: Right, bring him in.

[DEAN *is marched in by a* SOLDIER. *There is an uneasy pause.* DEAN *takes off his helmet, then his webbing. Pause. Finally he takes off his tunic. The* R.S.M. *and* SOLDIER *leave. The door is bolted.* DEAN *looks round the room and then sits at the table. He begins to write.*]

BILLY: My darling wife, May: Hope you are well. I know it's a long time since I've written, I've been in a bit of trouble. May, May, how can I tell you, how can I begin to explain? You wouldn't understand, I'm not the same Billy Dean that you married. When I married you, I was nineteen, I hadn't got a care in the world. Oh, May, if you could see me now, I'm 21 and I feel like 90, I'm old and tired. How can you be so old in two years, May? How the hell did I get here?

[*Pause.*]

Remember the day we saw the soldiers, we hadn't been married long, had we May? They came singing and marching past our street. It was exciting, all pals together, all going off to be soldiers. I wanted a part of that, May, me, Billy Dean, I wanted to be a soldier. Christ, May, I'll never forget the look on your face when you saw those soldiers.

[MAY *enters.*]

MAY: Oh, Billy, Billy, look, the soldiers are coming past. Come and look, Billy, come on!

BILLY: May?

MAY: Come and look Billy, quick, you'll miss them. Look, they're right the way down the park. Eh there's hundreds of 'em.

BILLY: Aye, its great, ain't it?

MAY: Eh, Billy, look! There's Jimmy Harris.

BILLY: Where? Where?

MAY: There, look at the end of the line. He's got a little tash. Hey, he looks good, doesn't he?

BILLY: Aye, he's a big lad now isn't he?

MAY: Eee, I wonder if his Mam knows he's joined up. She'll kill him! Oh Billy, look at the state of that one, his uniform's too big for him. Doesn't he look a sight?

BILLY: He works at the same place as me, him.

MAY: Eh, Billy, I couldn't 'alf fancy you in a uniform.

BILLY: Could you?

MAY: Yeah, you'd look smashing! Eh Billy, let's follow 'em. Come on! Look, there's a band an' all.

BILLY: No, May, stay, don't go yet.

MAY: Oh, yes, I want to go. C'mon, I'll race you.

BILLY: Don't go May, don't go.

MAY: Come on, Billy.

BILLY: Don't go, I need you!

MAY: Come on!

[MAY *exits.*]

BILLY: Those soldiers, they were like a breath of fresh air. Everyone was talking about the war, making speeches. Oh, there were some fine speeches, none as bloody fine as our Sergeant Major's. He stood there, a big bull of a man with a booming voice. All the men were listening to him. You couldn't get away, you just had to listen. He was talking to hundreds of people, May, but it seemed like he was just talking to me, I was the one he wanted.

[*During the above speech the* R.S.M. *has entered and taken up position.*]

R.S.M.: What I have to say is for the ears of all patriotic Englishmen: as you stand here in the safety and comfort of our
great nation, the war over in distant France goes on.
Your brothers, fathers, husbands, who have already
answered the call and taken up arms, risk their lives daily
to keep this great nation of ours free. For every Belgian
there are two Germans; for every Frenchman there are two
Germans, and for every Englishman there are two Germans.
But do our gallant lads swerve from their task? No, no,
because they are men — men who believe in fair play,
playing hard but playing fair. They believe in playing the
game, even when the odds are with the other side.
Our foes greatly outnumber our plucky comrades.
Their marauding hordes surge through France and Belgium,
raping women and carrying small babies on their bayonets.
Can you as Englishmen let this continue any longer? Who
can stand by and see innocent women and children fall
before the bloody bayonet of our foe? Who can stand by
and see our gallant lads fall in France's distant fields, because
it's in your hands, lads, it's in your hands. You can end
this war by enlisting today.
Now, who'll be the first man amongst you to take the
King's shilling?

BILLY: Me. I'll go.

[*The* R.S.M. *begins to whistle 'Tipperary'. The* PATRIOTIC
WOMAN *steps forward.*]

WOMAN: Mothers of English sons, can you stand by any longer
while your son lets others do his fighting for him, while he
earns for himself the hated name 'Coward'? Every day, out
there in fair France, hundreds of English boys are dying
needlessly. English mothers gave them: English mothers,
from the Queen to the cottager, sending their soldier lads
ungrudgingly to live or die for their Country. And your
boy is not there.
Why are our soldier boys falling so fast? Because the
might of the Hun is great and they are hopelessly outnum-

bered. But your boy is not there. You haven't sent him. I know myself what courage it takes to look into your darling's eyes and say "Go, my son!" But should we be faint-hearted when our men are fighting so bravely? We cannot fight. We cannot take up arms against our Country's foes. So we must give, give our boys, give freely and generously, with strong hearts that can bear the pain of parting for the sake of England.

Go home now, go to where 'he' is and say, as one English mother said recently to her son, "My boy, I don't want you to go, but if I were you I would go".

[MAY *has entered and heard the speech. She turns and goes to* BILLY.]

MAY: Billy, we can't ignore it any longer. All the men are going, and I can't hold you back. I was thinking, it would break my heart if anything happened to you. But that's selfish. All the other men are fighting for their country and that's where you should be. I don't want to lose you. But I'd be dead proud of you if you were a soldier.

BILLY: I don't want to lose you either, May, but I'm going. I've joined up.

WOMAN: [*Holds up a photograph.*] There's a man for you. Not afraid to lay down his life for his Country. I don't know how you slackers lounging about with cigarettes in your mouths have the gall to look my brave boy in the face.

MAY: I knew you would. I knew you'd go. You'll make a fine soldier.

BILLY: I'll miss you, May.

MAY: I'll miss you, too.

[MAY *and the* WOMAN *leave.*]

BILLY: You got me, didn't you, Sir? You asked for volunteers and I marched up, me and a thousand others like me. You wouldn't get me again so easily.

[*The* R.S.M. *turns and looks at* DEAN *and then exits.*]

You put us in uniform, taught us how to fight. Made men of us. Best time of my life, that. Out in the country all day, training to be a soldier. I'd never been out in the country before. Well I'd never been that far away from home before. Aye, best time of my life, all pals together, all soldiers. It was a game then, I wish it could have stayed that way.

> [TOMMY *enters. He takes off his pack, then takes out a small book and starts to read.*]

TOMMY: [*Mouthing*] Voulez-vous . . . [*He pronounces it how it looks.*]

BILLY: Tommy? What are you doing?

TOMMY: Learning French.

BILLY: What for?

TOMMY: We're going over to France, aren't we? They all speak it over there y'know. Yeah, they all speak funny. You want to see some of the words in here.

BILLY: Let's have a look.

> [TOMMY *shows him the book.*]

TOMMY: You can have it after me. All the words you need are underlined. Here, listen to this. Voulez-vous — good, eh?

BILLY: What does it mean?

> [TOMMY *thinks then looks in the book. He pulls a dirty face.*]

It means 'Will you?'

BILLY: Great!

TOMMY: Here! Here's another one. 'Une bouteille de vin'.

BILLY: What's that mean?

TOMMY: Where do you go on a Friday night?

BILLY: Down the pub for a pint.

TOMMY: That's what it means.

BILLY: What's the beer like over there?

TOMMY: They don't drink beer! No, everyone drinks wine. Picture it. You're in France, you've had a hard day digging trenches. The sun's burning down. Friday night comes around. What are you going to do?

BILLY: Go to bed.

TOMMY: Give over, Billy! I'm not going to France to sleep. We're going to have a good time. Go to a little French café. French waitress comes across. I smile at her, she smiles at me and I say "Une bouteille de vin".
[BILLY *goes to speak.*]
Hang on, hang on, I haven't finished! "S'il vous plaît." That means, 'a bottle of wine if you please'.
[*Pause.*]

BILLY: Here, I wonder what those French women are like.

TOMMY: Billy, you wouldn't believe it. They're not like ours, you know. No, they're — y'know — easy.

BILLY: Give over.

TOMMY: Oh yeah — Eh, you know when they kiss they . . .
[*He whispers in* BILLY'*s ear.*]

BILLY: No!

TOMMY: Yeah! Right down the back of your throat.

BILLY: I don't believe it!

TOMMY: Well, we'll soon find out, won't we, Billy?

BILLY: D'you have to learn everything in that book?

TOMMY: No — all you need is: "Où est ta mère?" That means, "Where's your Mam?" Then you say, "Voulez-vous promener avec moi?" That means, "Will you come for a walk with me?" But Sammy says you don't need all that, you just say, "Voulez-vous walkies?" [*He demonstrates with his fingers.*] Then when you're alone, this is the best one, you say, "Voulez-vous jig-a-jig?"

BILLY: What's that, Tom?

TOMMY: Give over Billy, man. You know 'jig-a-jig'!

BILLY: Oh. [*He doesn't get it.*]

TOMMY: I'll tell you, Billy, we're going to have a great time out there. [*Pause.*] Well, I'd better finish me letter. [*Pause. He starts writing.*] Eh Billy, how do you spell ceiling?

BILLY: Er . . . [*Pause.*] What do you want to spell that for?

TOMMY: How do you spell it?

BILLY: Why, what you writing?

TOMMY: I'm just writing to Doris and . . .
BILLY: Doris!
TOMMY: So what's wrong with Doris?
BILLY: Oh, nothing, nothing.
TOMMY: I'm just writing to tell her she'd better take a good look at the floor, because when I get home all she's going to see is the ceiling.
BILLY: How do you mean, Tom?
TOMMY: You know, 'jig-a-jig'.
BILLY: Oh! [*The penny drops.*]
TOMMY: How d'you spell it?
BILLY: S-E-A-L-I-N.
TOMMY: Thanks.

BILLY: Ah, Tommy, you were a daft sod. We never did make it to that French café, did we? It took them two years to train you and two minutes to kill you. Two minutes after we went over the top and you were dead. My, you were a good soldier, Tommy, best shot in the regiment, what a bloody waste.

BILLY: Where you going, Tommy?
TOMMY: We're on leave, aren't we? I'm going home like every other sod. I'm going to get the early train. What you going to do, stop here? Come on, get yourself shifted.
[TOMMY *exits.*]

BILLY: I couldn't wait for that leave to come along. That's why I got the early train home. Christ, May, the look on your face when you came home from work and saw me standing there.

[MAY *enters.*]
MAY: Billy Dean, what are you doing here?
BILLY: Hello.
[*He hugs her.*]

MAY: I thought you were getting the 8 o'clock train. I was going to come and meet you. I was going to put me best dress on and everything.

BILLY: Let's have a look at you.

MAY: Well?

BILLY: Beautiful. Come here.

> [*They hug.*]

MAY: Oh my — you've put on weight. You great fat thing. What have they been feeding you?

BILLY: Oh, they do you proud, meat and eggs for breakfast and that many spuds you can hardly eat them.

MAY: Oh well, I hope you're not expecting that here.

BILLY: Oh, I didn't come home to eat.

> [*He hugs* MAY *again.* ELSIE *enters.*]

BILLY: Elsie. Oh my God, Harry. Hello Elsie.

ELSIE: Hello, Billy. I didn't expect to find you 'ere.

BILLY: Aye, I'm on leave. I got the early train, thought I'd make the most of it. You're looking well. I was sorry to hear about your Harry. He was a good mate. How are you feeling?

ELSIE: I don't feel anything, Billy. I just hate.

BILLY: I know how it is, when I heard about your Harry I could have killed twenty Germans with me bare hands.

ELSIE: He's dead. Killing Germans won't bring him back. I can't help thinking there's some German woman feeling just the same as me now.

BILLY: I hope so.

ELSIE: It wasn't the Germans that killed Harry.

BILLY: They shot him Elsie.

ELSIE: It was the war. It's the war I hate.

> [*Pause.*]

BILLY: Don't go, Elsie.

MAY: Elsie, sit down, love. Don't stand there in the cold.

> [ELSIE *moves in and sits.*]

ELSIE: I didn't expect Billy to be back.

MAY: I know, nor did I. I just walked in and he was standing there as large as life. How're you getting on?

ELSIE: Oh fine. Everyone's helping out, you know. I've been sorting through everything. Mother's round helping. They sent me back his pay book. There was five shillings owing to him. I'll get a small pension, it seems, and with my wages we should be all right. Though what I'm going to do when the war's over and I can't work in munitions any more I don't know. Still, we'll cross that bridge when we come to it. I've been sorting through his things. He didn't have much. I've been going through everything. Most things I'm cutting down for the boys or selling. I'm selling his watch, I can get quite a few shillings for that — it all helps. But . . . er . . . I brought round his suit. Now don't say no straight away because I want you to have his suit, I think he would have liked that. I don't want to sell it and it's too good to cut up and I thought I'd take it round and offer it, and no offence or anything but I thought Billy Dean could do with a suit. He could use that. And as I say, it's a good suit.

BILLY: Yeah.

ELSIE: And he's not worn it much.

BILLY: I remember when Harry got that suit.

ELSIE: Aye. Well, I thought Billy Dean can wear that, he's not got a suit of his own.

BILLY: I've never had a suit.

ELSIE: There you are then. I don't know if it'll fit you because he was a big man, my Harry, but . . . er . . . it might do and anyway, May can always take it in for you, it's all lined you see, it's a properly tailored suit, that.

BILLY: It's a nice suit.

ELSIE: He saved up quite a while to get that. He was married in that. And I thought, well, it's no good me hanging on to it. No point in clinging onto the past or anything is there, really? Not going to be any use to me now. So I brought it round and as I say, I'd like you to have it.

BILLY: Thanks, Elsie.

ELSIE: Its not er . . . Well, it's a colour that can suit any man. It'll go with you. It'll look nice on you.

BILLY: I appreciate it.

MAY: It's lovely. Well, are you going to try it on? Go on.

[MAY *helps him on with it.*]

ELSIE: As I say, it's all lined round the sleeves . . . Well, that fits, doesn't it?

MAY: It fits lovely across the shoulders.

ELSIE: That looks very nice. Not too big for you at all. You must have been putting on weight.

MAY: Aye, he's fat.

ELSIE: Feeding you up in the army, are they?

BILLY: Aye, they know how to cook.

ELSIE: Yeah, it's not too big at all. It's very nice.

MAY: It's a long time since I've seen you in civvies.

BILLY: I'll have to watch out for the girls now, won't I?

MAY: Aye.

ELSIE: That's the suit I used to take down to the pawnshop every Monday morning. Fetch it out Saturday night so he could wear it on Sunday then take it back Monday morning to get a few shillings for the week. I reckon that's why it's so well preserved. They must have kept it in mothballs down there.

MAY: Are you sure we can't give you something for it, Elsie?

ELSIE: No, no, I said, didn't I? I don't want to sell it. That's a present.

BILLY: Thanks, Elsie.

[*He kisses her.*]

ELSIE: Pleasure.

[*Pause.*]

Oh, er . . . I'd better get off, leave you two alone, eh? You'll look fine walking through the park in that now.

MAY: Well, thanks ever so much.

ELSIE: I won't keep you any longer. Have a nice leave, Billy.

MAY: Aye, well, we'll see you later on for a drink maybe, will we?

ELSIE: Aye maybe. Bye-bye, anyway.

BILLY: Bye, Elsie.
ELSIE: Bye, Billy.
    [ELSIE *exits.* BILLY *takes off the coat quickly.*]
BILLY: Sell it.
MAY: What?
BILLY: Sell it.
MAY: Billy man, I can't sell it.
BILLY: Sell it and give the money to Elsie's kids.
MAY: I can't. Not when Elsie's brought it round for you.
BILLY: Sell it, I don't want it in the house.
MAY: Billy, that meant something, giving it to you.
BILLY: That's a dead man's suit May, now sell it, burn it, do anything you like with it but I won't have it in my house.
MAY: All right. All right, Billy. All right.
    [*She leaves with the suit.*]

BILLY: I hate the war. It's the war that killed Harry, not the Germans, Elsie, and I thought you were mad, I thought the shock had turned your brain, but you were right, I see that now. I just wanted to be a soldier that's all; and they made sure we were good soldiers.

    [*The* R.S.M. *marches* TOMMY *in.*]
R.S.M.: Left right, left right, left right. Training Company, halt! Right turn! Ground arms! Company will fix bayonets. Fix! Bayonets! Shun! At Ease. Horrible!
  To attack with the bayonet effectively requires good direction: strength and direction during a state of wild excitement, and probably physical exhaustion. [TOMMY *glances at him.*] Eyes front! The bayonet is essentially an offensive weapon. When you charge with a bayonet put on a killing face — that'll scare the shit out of Fritzie, and scream, I want you to scream hideously so your Missus can hear you back in Manchester — If you don't kill Fritzie, he'll kill you. So stick him between the eyes, in the throat, in the chest — don't waste good steel. Six inches are

enough. What's the use of a foot of steel sticking out the back of a man's throat? Three inches will do for Fritzie. When he coughs — go and look for another.

Remember, every Boche you kill is a point scored to our side. Every Boche you kill brings victory one minute nearer and shortens the war by one minute. So kill'em, kill'em. The only good Boche is a dead 'un. Now what's this 'ere? [*He points to a sandbag.*]

TOMMY: Sandbag, Sir.

R.S.M.: No it's not, it's a German, and don't you forget it. Fall in, Dean. [*Screams.*] Fall in, Dean! Where d'you think you are, on bleedin' holiday? Right Dean, let's see how you shape up with the bayonet.

BILLY: Haven't got a rifle, Sir.

R.S.M.: [*To* TOMMY] Give him your rifle.

[TOMMY *hands over his rifle and* DEAN *bayonets the sandbag.*]

R.S.M.: Do you know this feller?

BILLY: Who Sir?

R.S.M.: Fritzie here.

BILLY: No Sir.

R.S.M.: Well, anyone would think you loved the bloody swine, petting and stroking him like that. You're supposed to be killing him, not bleeding sleeping with him. Dean, you're about as useful as a one-legged man in an arse-kicking competition. Let's have another go, shall we, Dean? That's it, lad, that's better, hurt him now, that's right, in the belly, go on, tear his guts out, bite him I say, stick your teeth into him and worry him, go on, eat his heart out.

Give him back his rifle. Training Company shun!

[TOMMY *obeys and* BILLY *drops back.*]

Company will unfix bayonets. Unfix! Bayonets! Shoulder Arms. Right turn! Quick march! Left right, left right, left right. Pick those feet up you horrible man.

[*They exit.*]

BILLY: We wanted to fight. Hell, we never talked about anything else. We were frightened the war was going to be over by the time we got to France but it wasn't. It happened — Orders set for France. Final leave. Final leave: everybody singing, wishing you well. You came to the station in your best bib and tucker to see me off, May.
[MAY *has entered and stands looking out.*]
We had to wait an hour while they poured the wounded off an ambulance train.

MAY: Oh Billy, look at those poor men. That one's got no legs. He's shaking like a leaf.

BILLY: Don't worry about them, they get good treatment at the hospital. They're only the worst cases.

MAY: Well, this is it, then. It's come round really quickly, hasn't it?

BILLY: We've been lucky, May. Some of the men got shipped out to France straight away. We've had two years.

MAY: Aye I know, we've been lucky. I'll miss you, Billy.

BILLY: I'll miss you too, May. You keep making them shells, lass. We're going to need them when we get to France.

MAY: Aye, I will. Take care of yourself Billy, take care of yourself.

[*The* R.S.M. *and the* PATRIOTIC WOMAN *take up positions.*]

R.S.M.: You are being sent abroad as the soldiers of the King to help our French comrades against the invasion of a common enemy. This requires courage, energy, and patience. Remember, the honour of the British Army depends on your conduct. It will be your duty not only to set an example of discipline under fire but also to maintain the most friendly relations with those you are helping in this struggle.

You are going over to France, and consequently you'll meet a lot of French. You can do your own country no better service than showing the true character of a British soldier.

You cannot do this unless your health is sound, so keep constantly on your guard against any excesses — excesses both in wine and women. You must resist the temptations, and while treating women at all times with perfect courtesy, you should avoid any intimacy. Do your duty bravely, fear God and honour the King.

[*He whistles 'Tipperary' as the* PATRIOTIC WOMAN *starts her speech.*]

WOMAN: Girls! Your boy is leaving you to fight in the trenches. He's going to face some difficult times in his new life so give him a picture of you to carry away with him in his heart: a picture of something good and pure and straight and true that will help him in the trials ahead. He is a hero — be worthy of him.

Let us see no tear-filled eyes today, no trembling lips. However your heart may be torn with the parting don't let him down. Send him away with a cheery smile and a brave word. Come on, girls, keep your hearts up.

[*The* R.S.M. *and the* PATRIOTIC WOMAN *sing 'Tipperary'.*]

MAY: I'll be waiting for you, Billy, when you get back. I'll be waiting right here.

BILLY: Don't forget to write.

MAY: I won't. I'll write every day, and you write when you can. I know you won't get a chance very often but when you can.

TOMMY: Come on Billy, we're going to miss the train.

BILLY: All right, Tommy, I'll be with you in a minute.

MAY: Take care, Billy.

BILLY: I'll be all right, I can take care of meself.

[*All join in the singing — 'It's a long way to Tipperary but my heart lies there.' The* PATRIOTIC WOMAN *starts another verse.*]

R.S.M.: Fourteenth Platoon, fall in.

MAY: Well, bye then. I love you, Billy.

BILLY: I love you too, May.

MAY: Bye, Billy, bye.

R.S.M.: Fourteenth Platoon, fall in.
MAY: I'll be waiting for you.
[*The* PATRIOTIC WOMAN *hands* MAY *a Union Jack.*]
BILLY: Bye, May. Don't forget to write.
MAY: I won't. Take care of yourself, darling.
BILLY: Bye.
MAY: Bye, darling. I love you.
BILLY: I love you.
[*They join in the singing — 'It's a long way to Tipperary,'
etc., up to the last two lines.* MAY *and the* PATRIOTIC
WOMAN *wave flags. As soon as the song finishes,* MAY
and the PATRIOTIC WOMAN *leave. Pause.*]
R.S.M.: What's the matter with you lot! Anyone'd think you were
going to a bleeding funeral. Now come on, my lovely lads,
cheer up, I want you to sing. Sing for your nice Sergeant
Major. I want you to sing like little bleeding birds. [*Sings.*]
"Pack up your troubles . . ."
[*They join in and sing it twice through with mounting
pace and enthusiasm. The song finishes.*]

BILLY: What you stopped singing for, Tommy? Come on, Sir,
make them sing. Well, that's right, isn't it? Keep us singing, then we can't think.
[*The* R.S.M. *exits.*]
And we sang all right, all the way over to France, then
straight into the front line. Then the singing stopped,
didn't it? Why'd the singing stop, Tommy? Because
you're too bloody busy trying to keep yourself alive in the
front, that's why.
[TOMMY *kneels and puts on a steel helmet.*]
Aw, look at the state of you, Tommy, you're living in a
trench like a rat in a hole. All you can hear is the sound of
the guns pounding away. Can you hear the guns, Tommy,
and the flies, can you hear the flies feeding on the bodies of
your dead pals? Christ, sometimes you couldn't even hear
the guns for the sound of the flies.

Aye, Tommy you're just sitting there watching your dead pals turning grey, green, blue then black. The air's thick with the smell of rotten flesh.

That's right, Tommy, keep smoking the ciggies lad, it takes the smell away. You're up to your eyes in mud, aren't you, Tom? Everywhere covered in mud. All you've got to look at is two feet of blue sky. Keep down, Tommy, keep low. Don't stick your head above the trench, Tommy, you'll get it shot off. Keep low, Tommy, for Christ's sake keep your head down. Never stick your head above the trench in the same place twice or Fritzie'll have you.

Christ, Tommy, you can't even go to the lavvy in peace. You spend the nights freezing to death, listening to the guns pounding away — freezing — waiting for the dawn, dawn comes, guns stop. "Stand to, lads, wait for Fritzie to attack. Nothing doing today, lads, stand down. Guns stop, stand to, nothing doing, stand down, stand to, nothing doing, stand down, stand to, stand down, stand to, stand down." It's the same every bloody day, you're watching your mates getting shot to pieces and there's nothing you can do about it, just wait for Fritzie to attack.

Then it's different. We're not waiting any longer, we're going over the top, we're going to give Fritzie a taste of his own medicine. We're going to get our own back, Tommy, we're going over the top, we're going to kill Fritzie, we're going to tear his heart out. This is it, Tommy, it's our turn now.

[TOMMY *turns.*]

TOMMY: Aye, Billy, our turn now.

[*Pause.*]

R.S.M.: [*off*] Fix bayonets! Fix bayonets! [*building to a shout*] Fix bayonets!

[*During the dialogue:* "No Sir, Thomas is dead." "Jerry sniper." "The R.T.'s U.S., Sir." "That carrying party — move yourselves," etc.]

TOMMY: Look at the size of him.
BILLY: Eh?
TOMMY: Look at the size of it.
BILLY: Who? For Christ's sake, it's only a rat.
TOMMY: It's big as a bloody rabbit.
> [*He strikes at the rat with his rifle.*]
> You know what they reckon, Billy? You can get into a trench in Belgium, walk all the way through France into Switzerland and still be in the same trench. Funny that, isn't it? All they are is like big long graves.
BILLY: Shut up, Tommy.
> [*The* R.S.M. *enters and crouches in the trench with them.*]
> How long, Sir?
R.S.M.: Three minutes.
TOMMY: We haven't had any rum today, Sir.
R.S.M.: Rum carrier copped it. German snipper smashed the rum jar. No rum today.
TOMMY: Barbed wire's funny isn't it? I mean, all it is is bits of twisted metal. Loads of it out there, you know, barbed wire. I wonder who makes the stuff. [*Sings.*] "If you want to see a German soldier, I know where he is, I know where he is. If you want to see a German soldier, I know where he is . . . hanging on the old barbed wire." Here, Billy . . .
> [*The* R.S.M. *takes out his pistol.*]
> What did one spike say to the other spike?
BILLY: What?
TOMMY: Do you get the point!
R.S.M.: Make ready! Stand to!
> [*They all stand.*]
TOMMY: Jesus!
BILLY: I can't see a bloody thing!
> [*The* R.S.M. *blows his whistle. Screams from the* SOLDIERS.]

[*Blackout.*]

Men of East Yorkshire on newly won territory at Frezenburg, September 1917.

[*Lights up on* BILLY *and the* R.S.M. CAPTAIN HOWARD
enters.]

R.S.M.: Listen in. Shun!

CAPTAIN: At ease. Name?

BILLY: 13578 Dean, Sir.

CAPTAIN: Regiment?

BILLY: 18th Manchesters, Sir. 14th Platoon.

CAPTAIN: Now look Dean, I haven't got a lot of time, now tell me in your own words, as quickly as possible, what happened to you the day before yesterday when you went over the top at Trônes Wood.

BILLY: Well, the Sergeant Major blew the whistle and we went over the top of the trench. There was a lot of smoke from the shells and a lot of our lads were dropping but we kept moving forward, and then the lad on the right of me, Tommy Atkins, he was killed by a shell. The shell blast blew me down. When I got up . . .

CAPTAIN: Come on Dean, spit it out.

BILLY: . . . Well, I couldn't see anybody, Sir, because of the shell fumes so I couldn't find . . .

CAPTAIN: Stop. Sergeant Major, is this correct?

R.S.M.: Yes, Sir, visibility was very poor.

CAPTAIN: Thank you, Sergeant Major. Carry on, Dean.

BILLY: Well, I couldn't find me bearings, Sir. There was a lot of soldiers wandering around lost. Some of them had lost their rifles and helmets. Some of them had even lost their webbing.

CAPTAIN: Our chaps?

BILLY: Yes, Sir.

CAPTAIN: Your platoon?

BILLY: No, Sir. I think it was the 21st Brigade . . .

CAPTAIN: Enough. Very well, carry on.

BILLY: Well, some of these lads, they were caught in the cross-fire of the German machine-guns, and they were dropping like nine-pins, so I changed my direction.

CAPTAIN: What?

BILLY: I changed my direction, Sir.
CAPTAIN: You changed your direction? On whose authority?
BILLY: Well . . . mine, me own, Sir. There wasn't anybody else.
CAPTAIN: No Officer in charge?
BILLY: No, Sir. No Officer, no Sergeant, not even a Lance Corporal.
CAPTAIN: So you assumed this was a Jerry machine-gun post and changed direction.
BILLY: Well, it was, Sir, because . . .
CAPTAIN: To avoid it?
BILLY: Yes, Sir.
CAPTAIN: I see, Dean, carry on. Carry on, Dean, what happened next?
BILLY: I started moving forward, Sir. I still had me rifle and I jumped into a trench, and I heard voices, I thought it was the Germans at first but it was the 11th South Lancashire Pioneer Regiment.
CAPTAIN: Stop. You jumped into a trench?
BILLY: Yes, Sir.
CAPTAIN: One of our trenches?
BILLY: Well, I fell into it.
CAPTAIN: That would be Trônes Alley.
BILLY: Yes, Sir. That's where the Pioneers were. They were engaged in digging a fire-step.
CAPTAIN: Stop. Trônes Alley is half a mile back from Trônes Wood, isn't it? Is that correct, Sergeant Major?
R.S.M.: Yes, Sir. It's half a mile away from the position we attacked from.
CAPTAIN: Dean. Did you get a note from the Officer?
BILLY: No, Sir. I didn't think it was necessary.
CAPTAIN: Didn't think it necessary! Sergeant Major, any officer remember Dean being in Trônes Alley that day?
R.S.M.: No, Sir.
CAPTAIN: I see. Anyone else in that trench that you happened to see?
BILLY: I was digging a fire-step with a bloke called Chalkie.
CAPTAIN: Chalkie!

BILLY: That was his nick-name, Sir, they all called him Chalkie. Didn't know his real name.
CAPTAIN: This man, Sergeant Major?
R.S.M.: Dead, Sir.
CAPTAIN: Carry on, Dean.
BILLY: Yes, Sir. For the rest of the action I mucked in with these lads, digging a fire-step.
CAPTAIN: Come on, come on.
BILLY: Late in the afternoon we were relieved. We moved back to the brickworks, then I found that the 18th Manchesters had been relieved as well.
CAPTAIN: Stop. From the time you left Trônes Alley to the time you reached the brickworks you made no attempt to contact your Platoon?
BILLY: Couldn't Sir, there was too much shell-fire . . .
CAPTAIN: Enough. Carry on.
BILLY: Then I reported to the Sergeant Major, Sir, and he put me under arrest.
CAPTAIN: I see . . . I see, Dean, I see [*Pause.*] Now let's go through this again slowly. You set off from the front line.
BILLY: Yes, Sir.
CAPTAIN: You were knocked down. You saw a German machine-gun post, and you decided . . .
BILLY: Couldn't see it, Sir.
CAPTAIN: Well, you knew it was there — you assumed it was a German machine-gun post, and you tried to avoid it. In avoiding it you did a complete about turn and went backwards, arriving in our own trenches.
BILLY: I just thought . . .
CAPTAIN: You made no attempt while in this trench to regain your former position or regain your Platoon.
BILLY: No, Sir.
CAPTAIN: You place me in a very difficult position, very difficult. [*Pause.*] When did you enlist, Dean?
BILLY: 1914, Sir.

CAPTAIN: You were a volunteer.

BILLY: We all are.

CAPTAIN: That's right, Dean. The New Army consists of volunteers. The regular army does not consider the new army an efficient fighting force yet — we can't have chaps like you going backwards instead of forwards. We can't have people getting lost, we can't have people doing just what they like — it doesn't look good, Dean. Doesn't look good for the British Army. If your story is true. There are a lot of coincidences you would have me believe. You conveniently lost your Platoon during the first few minutes of the action.

BILLY: No, Sir.

CAPTAIN: Enough, Dean, I'm talking. Your Sergeant Major did not get lost, he carried on to your objective. You, Dean, did not. You avoided the machine-gun post of the enemy, and went back into your own trenches. Of the two people you say you saw in the trench, one is an officer whose name you can't remember, and the other is dead. And then after your chaps had been shot up . . . Do you hear me, Dean? Shot up . . . there's only five of them come back, we found you cosily hanging round the brickworks ready to report to your Sergeant Major. Were I to believe that, Dean, I could let you go, but I'm afraid it's not for me to judge — I'm going to have to forward it to a court martial, and you'll be judged by officers of your own regiment or any other of your own choosing. The charge is 'Cowardice in the face of the enemy'. The army cannot tolerate this kind of conduct. Dismissed, Sergeant Major.

[CAPTAIN HOWARD *exits.*]

R.S.M.: Listen in. Shun!

[BILLY *does not leave.*]

Right turn! Quick march!

[*The* R.S.M. *leaves.*]

R.S.M.: [*off*] Company! . . . Shun! Company!

[CAPTAIN HOWARD *enters. He reads.*]

CAPTAIN: Discipline Court Martial No. 1105. No. 13578 Private William Dean, 18th Manchester Regiment, was tried by Field General Court Martial on the following charge: 'Cowardice in the face of the enemy'. The sentence of the court is that he suffer death by being shot . . . the sentence to be carried out at 5.30 a.m., July 17th 1916. Company dismissed.

[CAPTAIN HOWARD *exits.* BILLY *stays.*]

[*Blackout.*]

END OF ACT ONE

Ruins at Contalmaison, September 1916.

Working for the war effort: women loading coke at the South Metropolitan Gas Works, Old Kent Road, London.

ACT TWO

BILLY *lights a candle and starts to write.*

Lights up on MAY *in the munitions factory.*

MAY: [*writing*] July 16th, 7 o'clock.
[*She reads through her letter while putting on her hat.*]
My darling Billy, hoping you are well as I am. I thought
I'd start this little note now and try and get it finished in
me breaks. I'm doing a night shift tonight.
[ELSIE *enters. She hangs up her shawl and starts to put
on her overall.*]
But don't worry, Elsie's here to look after me.

ELSIE: Not another letter. That poor boy must be up to his ears in
them by now, the number you send.

MAY: [*still writing*] He likes them. Oh my God, is it time?

ELSIE: Mmm.

MAY: Right, I'll have to finish this later now.
[*They start work.*]
Oh my God, Elsie, I'm that tired. I hardly got any sleep
today. Bloomin' kids were out in the street playing tin-tan-
alley-man at the tops of their voices.

ELSIE: Mother was trying to keep my lot quiet. Fat chance.

MAY: Is she looking after them tonight? Is she?

ELSIE: No, George.

MAY: Oh eh, he's getting his feet under the mat, isn't he? Be
moving in next!

ELSIE: Don't be so wet. He's very good with them. The boys love
him, especially Sammy. Thinks the world of him. Makes
him into a real hero.

MAY: Oh. It'll be a shame when he has to go. Has he had his call-
up papers yet?

ELSIE: Yes, they came last week.

MAY: Oh, Charlie Harris had his last week and he's got to go on Monday and he's got a hacking cough. Me dad says they'll be taking them with wooden legs next.

ELSIE: They're taking anything now. And he's married, Charlie Harris. It's hitting families hard now they're forcing men to go.

MAY: Aye, well, they need them. They need all the men they can get.

ELSIE: I remember when this factory was full of men. Now look at it. Three left. That's why they've got us here. 'Cos there aren't any men left. We're filling up dead men's places here.

MAY: Don't be so morbid. They're not all dead.

ELSIE: Did you see that man in the pub the other night? Sitting over in the corner. His hand was shaking so he couldn't hold his beer glass. He looked dreadful. Shell shock, that's what they're calling it. He'd no control. His nerves were all shot to pieces. He'll never work again, that feller.

MAY: I know, poor man. My God, these bullets. D'you know I dream about them?

ELSIE: Do you? So do I.

MAY: Yeah.

ELSIE: I'm packing bullets in me sleep now.

MAY: D'you know Elsie, no kidding, the other day I woke up and I was saying "More bullets, more bullets, more bullets."

[ELSIE *laughs.*]

ELSIE: I wonder how many we've made since we've been working here.

MAY: [*unthoughtfully*] Thousands.

[*They continue to work.*]

So when's George going, then?

ELSIE: He won't be going.

MAY: Why, is something wrong with him?

ELSIE: No, there's nothing wrong with him.

MAY: Well why isn't he going, then?

ELSIE: He says he's not going. He's sent back his papers. He's refusing to go. He says nobody's got the right to make his decisions for him.

MAY: Well, it's the same for everybody else.

ELSIE: He says nobody's got the right to tell him to kill men he doesn't want to kill, if it's against his conscience.

MAY: Oh, he's a conchie, then.

ELSIE: That's what they call them.

MAY: Don't you mind?

ELSIE: He's a good man, May.

MAY: People will say he's a coward.

ELSIE: Well, people can say what they like.

　　　[Lights fade.]

　　　[Lights up in a different area.]

R.S.M.: Fall in. You've all heard the sentence passed by Field General Court Martial — Private Dean is to be shot by firing squad at dawn tomorrow. This sentence has been confirmed by the Commander-in-Chief Field Marshall Sir Douglas Haig. The Officer in charge of the execution is Captain Howard. He has picked ten names at random from the remaining soldiers in this battalion: Prowse, Wood, Bromelow, Walsh, Green, Stirling. You six men will form the firing squad. You will hand your rifles in to me, cleaned and in good working order. At dawn tomorrow you will be handed your rifles back, each with a single round of ammunition, five rounds will be live, the sixth blank. You all know the reason for this. Walsh!

WALSH: *[off]* Sir!

R.S.M.: You will accompany me to the hut and escort the prisoner to the place of execution.

WALSH: *[off]* Sir.

R.S.M.: The remaining four names: Dunn, Faulkes, Sudlow, Nelson — you will act as stretcher-bearers and remove the corpse after the execution, and take it on a limber to a

place of burial. You will be informed of the exact where-
abouts later. The prisoner is locked up on the other side of
the farmyard. You will be billeted in this hut. You can
brew tea here and eat your rations. The owner of this farm
and his daughter know what's going on. If any of you men
come into contact with these people you will say nothing
— is that clear?

WALSH: [*off*] Permission to speak, Sir.

R.S.M.: What is it?

WALSH: [*off*] What's he doing?

R.S.M.: Writing a letter. Any more questions? Right, fall out!

[*The* R.S.M. *leaves.* WALSH *enters and moves into the
light.*]

WALSH: Walsh, you will accompany me to the hut and escort the
prisoner to the place of execution.

We're going to shoot Bill Dean tomorrow just because
he got lost. I wonder what they'd do if we all got lost . . .
All the corporals, all the sergeants, all the generals — if the
whole army got lost. I wonder what the Sergeant Major
would say. "Sorry we're late, Sir, but we got lost. Oh no,
Sir, not just me, the whole army got lost. What's that, Sir?
We're all going to be shot? If the whole army's going to be
shot, Sir, who's going to shoot us? [*Pause.*] Oh, I see, Sir,
we've all got to shoot ourselves. Sorry I was late. Bang!" —
the Sergeant would.

I could be home by now, doing me garden, planting
turnips. Nice row of turnips there, nice row of peas there,
Ivy on that back wall. No! Runner beans, just below 'em
potatoes. After all that hard work, down the road for a
pint. "Evening George, pint please, oh, nice head on it.
Well, Cheers! What's that George? Oh, we're growing
leeks in the trenches now, roses round the dugout, I'm
using my tin helmet as a hanging basket . . . celery in the
shell holes, sweet peas on the barbed wire. Oh yes, it's
very nice. The Germans? No, they mostly grow crocuses."

I wonder if the Sergeant Major's got a garden? He's

probably concreted it. We could all lay down our rifles tomorrow. "Here you are, Sir. We don't feel right about shooting Bill Dean, we're all going home. No, not just me, all of us. I'm going home to see my Missus. Well, cheerio! Bye for now and all that. Don't forget to write." They'd shoot us. They'd shoot us . . .

[*Pause.*]

"I don't think I should be on this firing squad, Sir . . . I know his family. I know his family."

[*Lights fade on* WALSH.]

[*Lights up on the munitions factory. It's tea break.* MAY *is writing a letter.*]

ELSIE: Aren't we talking, then?

MAY: I'm writing me letter.

ELSIE: Oh. [*Hands over a cup of tea.*] Tea.

MAY: I just can't understand it, Elsie. I can't understand how you can go out with a man like that.

ELSIE: A conchie, you mean?

MAY: Yeah.

ELSIE: I don't see him like that, see. He's just George to me, he's a person who happens to believe that what he's doing is the right thing.

MAY: Do you agree with him?

ELSIE: I respect him for what he's doing. He doesn't think it right to kill people. He doesn't believe in the war. Nor do I.

MAY: How can you not believe in it? Its happening — you can't ignore it.

ELSIE: I mean I don't believe it's right. It's been going on for two years now and it's just wasting our men. All those boys, just being wasted, for nothing.

MAY: It's not for nothing. How can you say that? How can you say it's for nothing? They're fighting for their country. Is that nothing! Does George think that's stupid, eh, to go and fight for your country? 'Cos I don't, I'm proud of them.

ELSIE: I was proud of them, too. I said the same as you. They're fighting for their country. I just never stopped to think what does that mean? What's the country ever done for them that they should fight for it? What was so precious about our lives before the war that we should all stand up and fight to protect it? What did you and Billy have?

MAY: We were all right.

ELSIE: You lived in those damp little rooms, poky little damp-walled rooms. Same as me and Harry. You had nothing. Nothing to call your own. The rooms weren't even yours, the furniture, the curtains, even the boots Billy had on his feet were second-hand. We were all the same. We had nothing. So what are we fighting for? To protect nothing!

MAY: Don't be daft. It's going to be better after the war. Course it is, that's why we're fighting. It's going to be a land fit for heroes. Everybody's saying. Plenty of jobs . . .

ELSIE: Yes, well, it's all very well providing jobs for them, only they won't be able to do the jobs half of them, they won't be able to work the machines! You've seen them, May. You've seen them coming back. They're wrecks. You saw that bloke in the pub. And they're the lucky ones. The rest of them are dead. So who's it fit for, this promised land?

MAY: It's for all of us, Elsie. It's for the kids growing up in the street. So when they grow up they can have a better life. That's what they're fighting for.

ELSIE: I just don't see how fighting Germans out in France is going to make our lives any better here. I don't see there's any guarantee our life's going to be any better for our kids than it was for us.

MAY: Look, Elsie, it would have been a damn sight worse if we hadn't stopped the Germans in their tracks, wouldn't it? Because they would have been over here. You saw what they did to Belgium. Well, it would have been the same here — the Hun marching down your street. Taking over and slaughtering people.

ELSIE: They're not monsters, May. They're only people like us.

They're as sick of it all as we are by all accounts. Do you remember what the soldiers said about Christmas when they were in the front line? They were sitting in the trenches and they saw this Jerry just walking across no-man's-land, and they couldn't believe it. And then they saw he had a bottle in his hand and he was shouting — "Happy Christmas, Tommy, come and have a drink with me." And then all along the line men were getting out of their trenches from both sides and meeting in the middle. They said they even had a game of football there. They were swapping photographs, sharing cigarettes, drink, and the Jerries said they were sick of the war, sick of the fighting, and they had nothing against us. And then orders came from both sides at once: that if the men didn't get back into their trenches the artillery would be ordered to start shelling them. Imagine that, May. Our own weapons what you and I sit here making, turned against our own men.

MAY: Oh, I don't expect they would have done it.

[*Lights down.*]

[*Lights on* BILLY *brighten. The* R.S.M. *enters.* BILLY *leaps to his feet. The* R.S.M. *puts a bottle on the table.*]

R.S.M.: Captain sent it, bottle of whisky.

BILLY: Thanks, I don't want it.

[*The* R.S.M. *offers* BILLY *a cigarette.* BILLY *refuses. The* R.S.M. *lights up.*]

Didn't know you smoked, Sir.

R.S.M.: Smoke too bleeding much. Writing to your sweetheart?

BILLY: Wife, Sir.

R.S.M.: Got a photograph?

BILLY: No, Sir, they took it away from me when they dumped me in here.

R.S.M.: Aye, they would.

BILLY: I'm trying to tell her what a bloody mess I'm in. Trying to write it all down so she'll understand. How can you explain to someone who hasn't been out here, hasn't seen the mess and the stupidity? I thought I knew why I joined up, I thought it was dead simple. We've got to stop the Germans. It's funny, isn't it, Sir, the only Germans I've ever seen are dead 'uns. Ever looked inside their wallets? They're the same as us, they've got wives, kids, play for the local football team, they've got mates, they even like drinking beer. They don't go round raping women and killing babies, they're just ordinary blokes like you and me. I wonder if they know why they're fighting.

R.S.M.: I read a poem once by a feller called Tennyson. He was a Lord or something. He wrote a poem called *The Charge of the Light Brigade*. It was about 600 men on horseback who were ordered to charge down a valley full of cannons — it was bloody suicide — a right cock-up. Hardly any of them came back. You know what this Lord Tennyson wrote of them? "Theirs was not to make reply, theirs was not to reason why, theirs was to do or die."

BILLY: Is that what you're gonna tell Tommy, whose body's rotting out there in no-man's-land, and the rest of the lads you trained to be soldiers, you gonna tell them that? You made us, Sir, you took us, a bunch of ordinary blokes and you made us into fighting men, you made us proud, strong, taught us to have respect for ourselves, for our regiment, for you.

When I went over the top, I wasn't thinking about no Germans, or King or Country. I wasn't even thinking about me Missus, Sir. I was thinking about you, and Tommy, and the rest of the lads, and not letting the side down, and I never. I never let it down. I kept going forward, just like you said. "Never go backwards, lads, always forwards." I just got lost. I got lost on the way to school once when I was a nipper, I got the strap for that. I made a mistake, I'm sorry I made a mistake.

Those officers who questioned me, they didn't seem to

understand. But you were there, Sir, you saw the smoke
and the shell fumes and the fallen trees, you know what it
was like. You were there. I just made a mistake, anybody
could have made a mistake out there. It was easy to make
mistakes, you couldn't see anything. You could have got
lost. Oh, I forgot, Sir, you never get lost do you? You never
make mistakes, you're just so bloody perfect, aren't you,
Sir?

R.S.M.: I joined this army when I was sixteen. Sixteen! Before that
there was four of us. Four of us and me mother living in
one room. We had nothing, we lived in a shit-heap. Then
sixteen comes along and I've got a chance to get out of it.
So I joined up. I lied about me age and joined up.

The army gave me rules to live by, hard rules, but good
rules, and God help you if you didn't obey them.

A lad I joined up with used to give our Sergeant Major a
lot of lip on parade. One day the Sergeant Major took him
behind the barracks and he beat the living daylights out of
him. He made us stand and watch him do it. Nobody ever
gave that Sergeant Major any lip again. They're good
rules, lad, as long as you obey them.

BILLY: But you're not going to beat the living daylights out of me
tomorrow, Sir, you're going to shoot me, you're going to
shoot me, Sir. Now why, why!

R.S.M.: Because there's a war on!

BILLY: Whose bloody war? It's not mine, I don't hate the Germans,
I don't hate anybody.

[*Pause. The* R.S.M. *makes to go.*]

Sir, tomorrow, in the morning, make sure there's no shaking
rifles. First time — no messing about, eh?

R.S.M.: Yes, lad.

BILLY: Pick the best shots, tell them I don't hold anything against
them, they're only following orders, aren't they?

R.S.M.: You'd best get on with your letter now.

BILLY: I want you to promise me something — don't tie me — I

don't want to be tied in the chair like an animal — promise
me, Sir.
[*Pause.*]

R.S.M.: Just get on with your letter.
[*The* R.S.M. *exits.*]

[*Lights up on* WALSH. *The* R.S.M. *enters.*]

R.S.M.: On your feet!
[WALSH *scrambles up and runs to the back.*]
Fall in. Squad, shun! At ease. In the morning the prisoner
will be placed in a chair. Privates Dunn and Faulkes —
you'll tie the prisoner's hands and feet to the chair, is that
clear? A blindfold will be placed over his eyes, and a piece
of white cloth will be pinned to his chest to assist as a
target. You will be told to 'present' and when the officer in
charge drops his handkerchief you will fire at the mark.
Now I want this done properly, no mistakes. If the lad's
not dead after you've shot him the officer in charge will
walk up to him, place his pistol to his ear and discharge a
bullet into him. Right. We'll try it now. Squad, shun —
present — take aim — fire!
[BILLY *hears these orders in the distance.*]
I only hope to God you shoot straight. Fall out.
[*The* R.S.M. *exits.*]

[*Lights up on the munitions factory.*]

MAY: Are you going to marry George?

ELSIE: I don't know. Maybe. I won't not marry him because he's
a conchie.

MAY: Have you thought what it'll be like? It'll be awful for you,
Elsie. The nasty things people'll say about you and the
way that they'll look at you in the street.

ELSIE: If you think that bothers me.

MAY: All right but what about your kids? What about them, eh?
What are you going to tell them when they come home

crying from school 'cos the other kids have been getting at them, 'cos they will, you know.

ELSIE: I'll tell them what I'm telling you. He's not a coward. He's a brave man and he's not going to do what he thinks is wrong because some snooty officer in a peaked cap tells him he should. He's not having that. And he's got the guts to stand up to that bloke who's got all that power and say, no, I'm not going. And they're making 'em suffer because they don't like that. They're putting them in prison for it. There's talk of them sending them to France and out there if they won't fight they can shoot them — and that's what he's facing!

MAY: Your Harry died out there Elsie. And my husband's out there risking his life right now. And don't think I don't want him home safe as well, 'cos I do. I don't want him getting shot at. I worry about him all the time. I lie awake at night worrying about him.

ELSIE: That makes two of us then, May.

MAY: I just wish the war was over. I just wish it was all over.

ELSIE: I haven't forgotten Harry, you know. I'd never forget him. But I'm only 27 and I've got to go on living.

[*Lights fade.*]

[*Lights up on other area.* WALSH *enters and then the* R.S.M.]

WALSH: That you, Sir?

R.S.M.: What you doing out here?

WALSH: Just come out for a breath of air, Sir.

R.S.M.: What are the other lads doing?

WALSH: Most of them are playing cards, Sir. Cold out here, isn't it, Sir?

R.S.M.: How long you been over here?

WALSH: Couple of months, Sir.

R.S.M.: You should have been here in the winter of '15. Weren't here then — still back in Blighty.

WALSH: Yes, Sir.

R.S.M.: I found one lad on sentry duty after a real cold night. Thought I'd caught him asleep. Just about to kick him up the arse — eyes were wide open. Face grey — he was stiff as a board — had to prise his rifle out of his 'ands. Couldn't make a fire — all you could do was stamp your feet up and down. Not allowed to take your boots off to rub your feet — wouldn't be able to get 'em back on again — too stiff. Bully beef — frozen into blocks — tea froze in seconds. Some of the lads tried to shove newspapers inside their shirts to keep warm. Put on extra layers of clothing. Pullovers, balaclavas, socks their wives and sweethearts had knitted them but that bloody cold still got in. Still chilled your bones. But when the sun came up in the morning like a big yellow ball over no-man's-land and you felt the warmth of it hit your face . . . Hadn't you better be going in then, lad?

WALSH: I don't think I should be in this firing squad, Sir. You see, I know him — Bill Dean.

R.S.M.: We all know him.

WALSH: No, you don't understand . . .

R.S.M.: This is not your responsibility, lad. It's somebody else's.

WALSH: But I know his family.

R.S.M.: The responsibility doesn't lie with you, it lies elsewhere! [*Pause.*] You'd better go and see to your rifle.

> [WALSH *exits. The* R.S.M. *looks at his watch and follows.*]

> [ELSIE *and* MAY *are sitting finishing off work.*]

MAY: Well, that's me finished.

ELSIE: That's the lot.

MAY: Oh, I can hardly keep my eyes open. I can't get this lid on, Elsie.

> [ELSIE *does it for her.*]

Oh, ta.

ELSIE: You get yourself sorted. I'll sweep up this morning.
[*She starts sweeping.*]

MAY: Oh, thanks Elsie. Oh, don't let me forget to post this letter
to Billy on the way home — we'll have to go down Cross
Street. [*As she says this she takes the letter from her pocket.*]
Oh, my God, Elsie.

ELSIE: [*still sweeping*] What?

MAY: I've just felt in me pocket.

ELSIE: What?

MAY: Look. [*She holds out a match.*] It must have been in me
pocket all night.

ELSIE: What d'you want to bring a match in for?

MAY: I didn't know it was there. I must have put it in with me
comb.

ELSIE: My God, if that had fallen out of your pocket and somebody had scuffed it.

MAY: Oh, what am I going to do if somebody catches us?

ELSIE: Well, stop waving it about, put it away.

MAY: Where.

ELSIE: Put it in your hanky.

MAY: Oh, come on Elsie, let's get out of here. Let's just put our
things on and go before somebody comes round.

ELSIE: No. It'll look odd if we leave early. Look, put that thing
away and just stand there while I just finish this sweeping.
[*She starts sweeping again.*]

MAY: I never knew it was there.

ELSIE: You heard what happened in that other workshop to that
Alice —

MAY: What?

ELSIE: She's in prison for bringing in a match.

MAY: You're joking.

ELSIE: She just pulled out her handkerchief and a match fell out
of her pocket. The forewoman was there. They took her
away. Where've you put it?

MAY: In me sleeve.

ELSIE: Well, don't hold it, it looks obvious . . . Said the whole place could have gone up. They said it didn't matter whether she did it on purpose or not — they had to make an example of her so that nobody'd ever do it again. She's sitting in Strangeways now — in a right state — she's only sixteen. Come on, get your shawl on — let's get out of here. Don't look so worried.
[*Lights out.*]

[BILLY *is writing furiously at the table. The door opens. The* R.S.M. *and a soldier enter and face him.*]
R.S.M.: On your feet, soldier.
[BILLY *rises and falls to the feet of the* R.S.M.]
BILLY: Please don't let them shoot me. I don't want to die.
R.S.M.: [*to* SOLDIER] Get him on his feet . . . get him on his feet. Don't make this difficult for us.
[*They turn and leave. Pause. As we wait for the shots* MAY's *laugh breaks the silence.*]

[ELSIE *and* MAY *move into centre light.*]
MAY: Oh my God, Elsie.
ELSIE: No May, but it's serious.
[*They laugh.*]
MAY: Eee, I know. No, it is, though, Elsie — the whole place could have gone up.
ELSIE: I know.
[*They laugh.* MAY *takes the match out of her pocket.*]
MAY: Eee, Elsie.
ELSIE: Just that one little bugger.
MAY: Thank God I got away with it!
[*She throws the match over her shoulder. They both laugh.*]
Come with me while I post me letter, you.
[*They leave, arm in arm.*]

[The R.S.M. *enters. He takes* BILLY's *letter and burns it. Simultaneously* WALSH *enters and takes out a diary and writes:*]

WALSH: July 17th, 1916 . . . This morning we shot Bill Dean . . . It was raining . . . We're moving up to the front tomorrow . . .

THE END

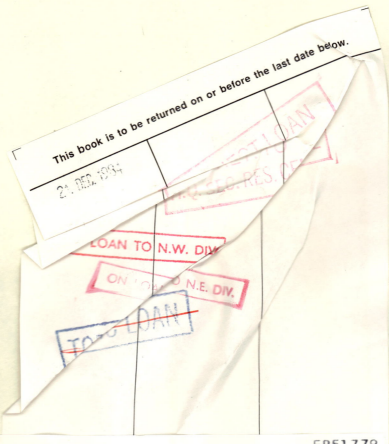